James I (1566–1625) — Anne of Denmark (1574–1619)

Charles I (1600–49) — Henrietta Maria of France (1609–69)

Elizabeth (1596–1662) — Frederick V (1596–1632)

Henry Frederick (1594–1612)

Charles II (1630–85) — Catherine of Braganza (1638–1705)

Sophia (1630–1714) — Ernest Augustus Duke of Brunswick (1630–98)

George I (1660–1727) — Sophia Dorothea of Celle (1666–1726)

George II (1683–1760) — Caroline of Anspach (1683–1737)

Caroline (1712–57)

Amelia (1711–86)

Anne (1709–59) — William IV of Orange (d 1751)

Frederick Lewis (1707–51) — Augusta of Saxe-Gotha (1719–72)

George III (1738–1820) — Charlotte of Mecklenburg-Strelitz (1744–1818)

Augusta (1737–1813) — Charles of Brunswick (1735–1806)

Edward (1767–1820) — Victoria of Saxe–Coburg (1786–1861)

William IV (1765–1837) — Adelaide of Saxi-Meiningen (1792–1849)

Frederick Duke of York (1763–1827) — Frederica of Prussia (1767–1820)

George IV (1762–1830)
Maria Fitzherbert (1756–1837) — Caroline of Brunswick (1768–1821)

Victoria (1819–1901) — Albert of Saxe-Coburg (1819–61)

Charlotte (1796–1817) — Leopold of Saxe-Coburg (1790–1865)

Edward VII (1841–1910) — Alexandra of Denmark (1844–1925)

Victoria Adelaide (1840–1901) — Frederick III (1831–88)

Albert Victor Duke of Clarence (1864–92)

William II German Emperor (1859–1941) — Augusta of Schleswig-Holstein (1858–1921)

Edward VIII (1894–1972) — Wallis Warfield Simpson (b 1896)

Elizabeth II (b 1926) — Philip Mountbatten Duke of Edinburgh (b 1921)

Anne (b 1950) — Mark Philips (b 1950)

Charles, Prince of Wales (b 1948)

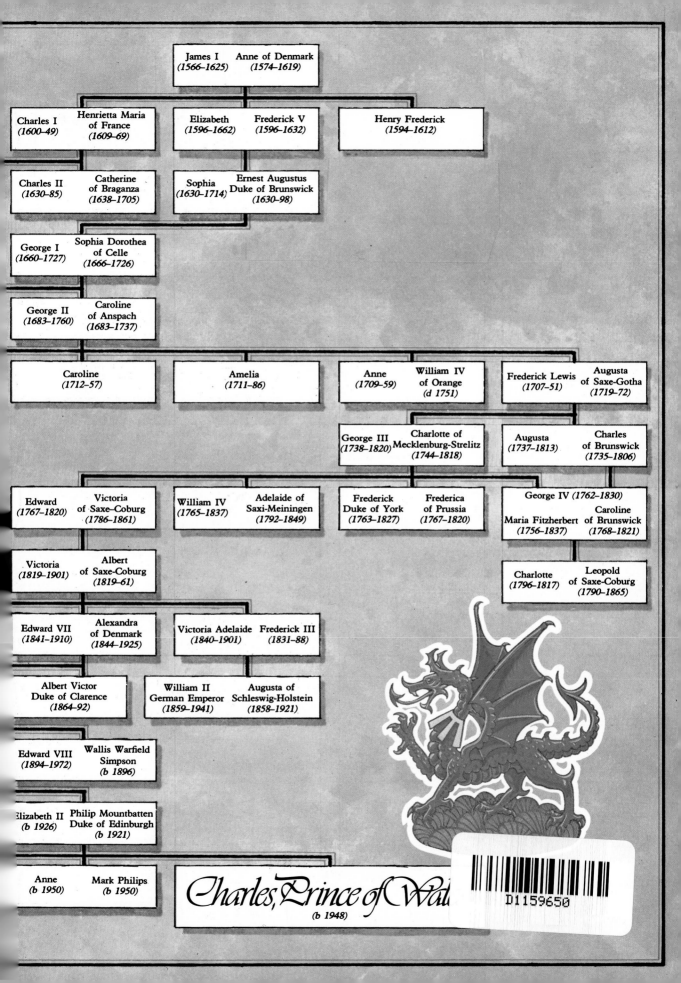

The world was delighted when, on 24th February 1981 after years of speculation, the heir to the throne of England announced his engagement to a truly charming bride: 19-year-old Lady Diana Spencer.

PURNELL

Brenda Ralph Lewis

ISBN 361 05238 3
Copyright © 1981 Purnell and Sons Limited
Published 1981 by Purnell Books, Berkshire House,
Queen Street, Maidenhead, Berkshire
Made and printed in Great Britain by Purnell and Sons
Limited, Paulton (Bristol) and London
Colour reproduction by K.L.W. Plates Ltd., London

When Prince Charles Arthur George, first son of the then Princess Elizabeth and Prince Philip, was born on 14th November 1948 at Buckingham Palace, the event was celebrated with blue – for a boy – floodlighting in London's Trafalgar Square. Charles, photographed (right) aged one month by Cecil Beaton and below showing an early interest in music, was by lineage a truly international Prince, with English, Scottish, Danish, German, Dutch, French and Russian blood in his veins. The young Prince lived in Clarence House, and his nurse often pushed his pram around the nearby parks (opposite, left). Under the watchful eye of his mother, the two-year-old Prince watches a procession from the walls of Clarence House (opposite, below). Charles and his sister, Princess Anne, spent their holidays at Balmoral. Opposite, top right, they are greeted at the local station, Ballater, in 1953.

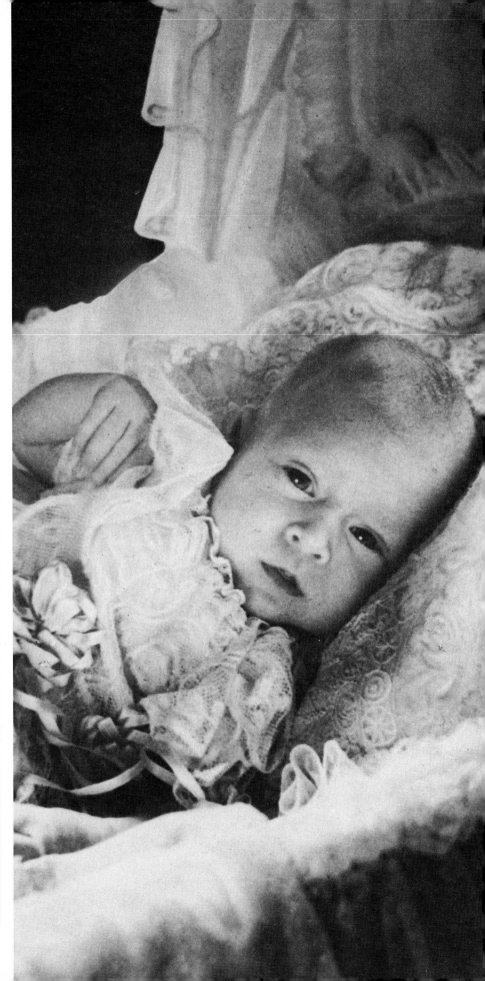

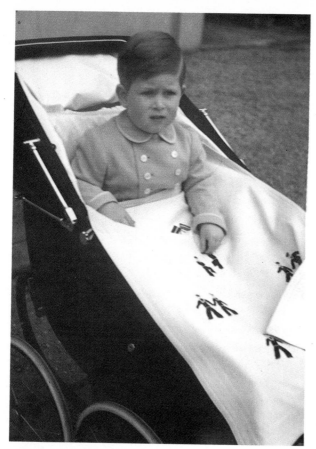

he delightful 20-year-old who married Prince Charles on 29th July 1981 had to fit a pretty demanding bill before she became the first Princess of Wales for over eighty years. And the fact that she fits that bill so well, and has been greeted into the Royal Family and the nation's heart with such unstinting approval is as much a matter for celebration as the marriage itself.

For the field from which Charles was able to choose his bride was a narrow one. No heir to the English throne can, by law, marry a Catholic, and there was a distinct shortage of the ranks of princesses from which princes once sought their wives. This, and his own wish to marry 'someone British', always made it more likely that Prince Charles would marry a commoner, but a commoner who could become a Princess of Wales and future Queen are not all that common. Potential candidates have put themselves literally out of the royal court merely by saying the wrong thing in public, or failing to cope coolly with the pressures of being in the public eye. In addition, world's most eligible bachelor or not, not all the girls rumoured to be in the running were in love with Prince Charles. And a love match has always been the greatest 'must' of all.

The girl who passed all these tests with such flying colours was born on 1st July 1961, the third daughter of the 8th Earl of Spencer and his first wife, the former Hon. Frances Roche. As a child, Lady Diana Frances Spencer spent most of her time at Park House, on the Queen's Sandringham estate in Norfolk, where she became the childhood chum of Prince Andrew and Prince Edward. Prince Charles took on the role of admired though not remote elder brother, and he remembers Diana from those days as a 'rather splendid' 16-year-old, full of fun and bounce and with a warm, infectious laugh.

At sixteen, Diana left school and went on to finishing school in Switzerland. She was there a mere six weeks. The artificial atmosphere of the school and the social whirl for which its pupils were trained was not for a girl who loves the outdoor country life and its sports, hobbies like reading, ballet and music, and who shares with Prince Charles a dislike of pomposity: both, in fact, have a penchant and ability for mimicking stuffy officials. Much more in the Princess's line was the work she eventually took up as a kindergarten teacher, where she showed a natural ability for getting on with young children.

A girl of this unpretentious and affectionate nature was clearly compatible with a thoughtful Prince who has a strong sense of romance and a deep interest in people and their problems and welfare.

The outgoing and adventurous 'Action Man' Charles of today was, surprisingly, somewhat shy as a boy. The Queen and the Duke of Edinburgh's choice of schools for their son was designed, it seems, to toughen Charles up – Cheam, Gordonstoun in Scotland, and during 1966, Timbertop and Geelong in Australia, where Charles lived something of a back-to-nature, pioneering life. He loved every minute of it, and it gave him a new confidence. He went on to become the first member of the Royal Family to take a University degree, at Cambridge.

In 1969 Charles was invested Prince of Wales at a magnificent ceremony at Caernarvon Castle. The day of Prince Charles' investiture, 1st July 1969, happened to be Diana's birthday, and naturally no one dreamed that his future wife was then blowing out eight candles on her birthday cake. Plenty of people had speculated, however, and Prince Charles was 'married off' in rumour at least eight times before he turned eleven, and the rumours multiplied as he grew older.

After his remark that thirty was a good age for a man to marry, Charles' own thirtieth birthday, 14th November 1978, was attended by feverish speculation about his friendship with Lady Sarah Spencer, the Princess's elder sister, but Lady Sarah said she was not in love with Charles, although she thought him 'a fabulous person'.

'I do not believe,' Lady Sarah said, 'that Prince Charles wants to marry yet. He still has not met the person he wants to marry.'

But he had. He just didn't know it until August 1980 when Lady Diana Spencer, just turned nineteen and very attractive, graceful and unaffectedly charming, came to spend a weekend at Balmoral. This was nothing new for Diana, whose family is closely connected with the Royal Family. Her father, for instance, was once the Queen's Equerry, and both her grandmothers were firm friends and Ladies in Waiting to the Queen Mother. The closeness was such that Diana used to call the Queen 'Aunt Lilibet'. That weekend in August 1980, however,

Opposite, Prince Charles on his fifth birthday. By this time, his mother had succeeded as Queen Elizabeth II and Charles was heir to the throne.
The Royal Family has always been close and affectionate. Charles is seen (right) with his beloved grandmother, the Queen Mother, and his aunt, Princess Margaret, at Balmoral in 1953. In 1954, he accompanies Great-Uncle Dickie, Lord Mountbatten, (below) after disembarking from the Royal yacht Britannia *in Malta.*

Charles and Diana walked, talked, went fishing together, and it seems that suddenly there was a new seriousness in their relationship. When Diana returned to her London flat, Charles telephoned her, using a secret code. A bunch of red roses followed.

The Press, alerted to the new royal romance in September, headlined it: IN LOVE AGAIN: IS IT THE REAL THING FOR CHARLES AT LAST? The fact that it was, indeed, the 'real thing' was for some time obscured by a barrage of denials, and protests about the way the Press were literally pursuing Diana. They camped outside her London flat, and descended in hordes on the nursery school where she worked.

The Princess herself appeared remarkably unrattled by the fuss, and showed considerable aplomb and cool-headedness in dealing with the endless questions fired at her by reporters and the ceaseless clicking of dozens of Press cameras.

Though nerve-racking, the experience completed the picture of the highly suitable bride the Princess has made for Prince Charles. Charm, good looks, respectability, mutual interests and an affectionate nature were joined by dignity and level-headedness – a perfect recipe for a Princess of Wales and future Queen whose life

The Royal Family has always enjoyed the outdoor, and particularly the sporting life. They all share an interest in horses. The Badminton Horse Trials are among several events which are a regular 'must' for the Royal Family. Prince Charles and the Queen are shown (opposite) attending the Badminton Trials of 1961. Both Charles and his sister Anne have followed in the Queen's footsteps and have become excellent horse riders. Charles is particularly known for his ability at polo, and Princess Anne has represented Great Britain several times in three-day events. Her husband, Captain Mark Phillips, is also a keen rider of international standard. By the time Charles attended Badminton in 1961, he had a new brother, Prince Andrew, who was born in 1960. Twenty-one years later, Prince Andrew, together with their youngest brother, Prince Edward, acted as Prince Charles' attendants at his wedding. Prince Andrew carried the wedding ring.

As a royal Prince and the heir to the throne, Charles grew up in the public eye, and soon became accustomed to formal occasions. Even as a young boy, Charles took his public duties calmly. At the Braemar Games in 1964, when he was sixteen, Charles looks relaxed and happy as he greets the officials before getting into his car (above). Some occasions are less formal, however, such as the summer event attended by a rather thoughtful young Prince (above left), followed by his mother, the Queen, and his grandmother, the Queen Mother.

The Royal Family are a close family and always like to celebrate special occasions together, whenever their busy schedule of engagements at home and abroad allows. Left, the Queen and Prince Philip and their family, Prince Charles, Princess Anne, Prince Andrew and Prince Edward, pose in Buckingham Palace for the official photographs on the occasion of the Queen and Prince Philip's Silver Wedding Aniversary in 1972.

The Princess of Wales has two older sisters, Lady Sarah, born in 1955, and Lady Jane, born in 1957. Her brother Charles, Viscount Althorp, was born in 1964. In April 1978 the Princess was a bridesmaid at Lady Jane's wedding (above right). Above, the Earl of Spencer (then Viscount Althorp) and the former Hon. Frances Roche at their daughter's christening. Below, Earl Spencer in the wine shop at his Althorp estate where he lives with his second wife, Lady Dartmouth. The young Princess with her guinea-pig Peanuts at the 1972 Sandringham Show (opposite), and enjoying a camel ride with her brother as a birthday treat (right).

will, of necessity, be lived largely in the extremely curious public eye.

The key to the whole thing, of course, was the fact that Diana was very much in love with Prince Charles and he with her. This was very obvious on 24th February 1981 when at long last all the rumours came to an end and the world's most eligible bachelor formally announced his engagement.

Interviewed on television that day, Prince Charles said that after he proposed to Diana over a candlelit dinner, he suggested that she think things over on a forthcoming twelve-day visit to Australia, in case 'it was going to be too awful.' Diana went to Australia, but she had no need to think things over.

'I never had any doubts about it,' she said on her engagement day.

Five months later, the world saw her as the radiant bride of a happy bridegroom at St Paul's Cathedral, and had no doubts about it, either.

On 25th May 1978, Charles received the robes and insignia of the Order of the Bath (below) at Westminster Abbey, London. Behind him is another member of the order, his great-uncle Lord Louis Mountbatten. Charles' public duties take him all over the world. In 1980 he toured India. He looks equally relaxed talking to officials at Delhi airport (centre right) where he arrived in full naval uniform for an official reception, and chatting to the Indian people (centre) on one of his informal walkabouts during the tour. Charles, and all the members of the Royal Family, enjoy the chance to meet and talk to people in informal situations, although their security men must be constantly on the alert.

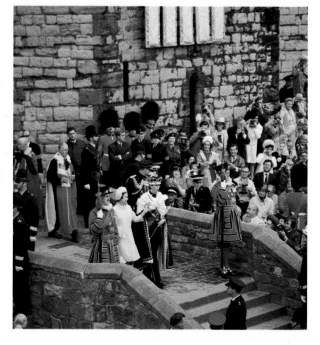

Another public duty is inspecting troops. Again in naval uniform, Prince Charles performs this duty at the restored Prince of Wales Bastion, a fortress on St Kitts Island, in 1973 (above). Charles was invested as the 21st Prince of Wales at a magnificent ceremony at Caernarvon Castle on 1st July 1969 (left; opposite, top and bottom). The tradition by which the eldest son of the English monarch becomes Prince of Wales goes back to 1284, when King Edward I presented his newly-born son, also Edward, to the newly-conquered people of Wales. Their last native Prince of Wales, Llewllyn ap Gruffyd, an ancestor of Prince Charles through the Welsh-born King Henry VII, had been killed in battle in 1282. Since then, only two English Princes of Wales have been invested at Caernarvon: Prince Edward, the future King Edward VIII and Duke of Windsor, in 1911, and Prince Charles. The Queen happily presents her heir to the Welsh people (left) from the battlements of Caernarvon Castle. Prince Philip looks proudly on. Below them hangs a banner with the Prince of Wales' ostrich feathers and motto 'Ich Dien' (I serve). The first Prince of Wales to wear these was Edward, the Black Prince, in 1346.

A life on the ocean wave is
nothing new in the Royal
Family. Charles'
great-grandfather, George V,
the 'sailor King', grandfather,
George VI, his father, Prince
Philip and 'Uncle Dickie'
Mountbatten were all naval
men. Mountbatten, who had an
extremely distinguished naval
career in the Second World
War, once remarked that: 'Life
in the Royal Navy is a
marvellous training for a future
king.' The future King of
England, suitably bearded, is
shown (opposite, top centre)
giving commands as captain of
the minesweeper HMS
Bronington, in 1976, and being
welcomed ashore in Barry,
Wales (opposite, centre) by an
enthusiastic crowd of
well-wishers.
Helicopter and jet aircraft flight
training were part of Charles'
RAF and naval training. He
takes the controls of a RN
Wessex 5 Commando helicopter
(opposite, top left). This was a
case of like father, like son, for
the Duke of Edinburgh is also a
qualified helicopter pilot.
Charles' brother, Prince
Andrew, also qualified as a
helicopter pilot in 1981. Charles
scored a royal first, however,
when he became the first member
of the Royal Family to make a
parachute jump (opposite, top
right). Charles was on a
training jump on 29th July 1971
from an Andover aircraft at
Studland Bay, Dorset. Charles
later admitted that this had been
terrifying enough, but the
arduous commando assault
course he took at the Royal
Marine Training Centre at
Lympstone, Devon (opposite,
bottom left) was even more so: 'a
most horrifying expedition',
Charles called it.
Prince Charles joined the Royal
Air Force (left) in March 1971
and trained at the RAF College
at Cranwell as a
Flight-Lieutenant.
At the Army College, Sandhurst
(opposite, bottom right) he took
the salute at the 1978
Sovereign's Parade.
In December 1976, when he left
the Royal Navy and Royal Air
Force, Charles was promoted an
RN Commander and an RAF
Wing Commander.

The Princess of Wales' coming-of-age in 1979 was marked by a typically charming photograph taken by the Earl of Snowdon (opposite).
Pictured on this page is Diana the working girl, at the Young England kindergarten at St Saviour's Church Hall in London's Pimlico. A close, affectionate family like the Royal Family were naturally delighted to see the Princess's own fondness for children. In addition to working at the school, where she cared for fifty children and gave them some elementary education, Diana spent one day a week looking after the child of a close friend of hers.

Prince Charles is a real sports enthusiast. He began playing polo in 1962. The game, which originated in India, requires skill, nerve, accuracy and is not without its dangers. Perhaps that is why Prince Charles' polo coach Sinclair Hill is one of the few people allowed to swear at him! Charles is shown in action on the polo field at Windsor Great Park (above and right) and doing a quick change into polo gear at Cowdray Park (far right). Charles made his flat racing debut (below) at Plumpton, Sussex in 1980 on Long Wharf.

Prince Charles goes to
Deauville each summer to play
with a polo team called Les
Diables Bleus – the Blue Devils.
In 1980 he visited Palm Beach,
Florida to watch the opening
round of the World Cup polo
tournament (far left).
The Prince also enjoys sailing,
and in 1967 was crewman for
Uffa Fox when they competed at
Cowes in the yacht Labrador
(top).
Come winter, come winter sports
for the Prince: skiing is another
of Prince Charles' sporting
activities. He is shown (left) on a
skiing holiday at Klosters in
Switzerland. Torchlight
tobogganing down the slopes
(above) is also in Prince
Charles' line. Winter sports is
one of the many interests shared
by the Prince of Wales and his
new Princess, who is an
accomplished skier.

Prince Charles loves the outdoor life, as does his new Princess. A thoughtful, kilted Charles admires the scenery at Balmoral (right) and dances an impromptu jig with his young cousin, Lady Sarah Armstrong-Jones, daughter of Princess Margaret (opposite, centre left). Among many entertainments devised for his young cousins, Charles wrote a fairy story The Old Man of Lochnagar. Illustrated by Sir Hugh Casson, it was published in 1980 and topped the bestseller lists.

Charles starts off on a trek to the Himalayan foothills (below) in December 1980 during his official tour of India and Nepal. With the Prince is a Nepalese sherpa, one of several who acted as guides for the Prince.

Opposite, top left, Charles occupies the first pilot's seat at the controls of a jet arriving at Esperance in Western Australia in 1979.

Charles tries his hand at fly fishing (opposite, centre right) and archery (opposite, bottom left). In Australia in 1979, he also enjoyed wind surfing (opposite, bottom right), which is a difficult skill to master.

Charles was especially close to his paternal great-uncle Lord Mountbatten (opposite, top right seen chatting to the Prince) and at the Memorial Service after Mountbatten's tragic and violent death in August 1979 was seen to shed a silent tear.

The £100,000 flat which the Earl of Spencer bought for his daughter (right) was virtually besieged by reporters and cameramen when the news of the romance of Charles and Diana became known to Fleet Street in September 1980. By November, when an announcement was expected for Prince Charles' 32nd birthday – it was never made – speculation had reached fever pitch. The Princess kept her cool in admirable fashion and complained only that the fuss, which also had the Press camping outside the Pimlico kindergarten where she worked, was disturbing her work with the children. Opposite, the Princess with two of her charges. These pictures of the Princess were taken at this trying time. On one occasion in November, Diana fumbled the doorlock of her car and stalled the engine (below), but otherwise she kept her nerve remarkably throughout the difficult situation.

Behind the scenes, though, the royal romance grew, and the couple managed to spend quiet weekends together away from the prying eyes and constant pressure of the Press. All rumours were strenuously denied by the Royal family. Nevertheless, the romance remained hot news, and reached its peak when Diana drove to Buckingham Palace on 23rd February 1981 and spent two and a half hours there. Speculation ended and congratulations began on the following day.

Engagement Day, and Prince Charles and his charming new fiancée face the Press. 24th February 1981 was, fortunately, an unseasonally fine day, and the newly engaged couple met the swarms of Press photographers and journalists in the gardens behind Buckingham Palace. Diana was wearing an attractive blue suit and a royal blue ring (below). Made by Collingwoods of Conduit Street, London, it featured a beautiful sapphire surrounded by diamonds. Soon after, similar rings were on sale all over the country. These were the pictures which were being produced in hairdressing salons everywhere as the new, fashionable 'Lady Diana Hairstyle' was copied. Australians went even further: they held a Lady Diana Look-Alike competition and the winners met Prince Charles when he arrived there on his five-week, four-nation tour in April.

From engagement day onwards, the Princess-to-be came 'under the protection' of the Royal Family. She left her Earl's Court flat and took up residence with the Queen Mother at Clarence House until the wedding.

Charles and Diana were very busy before their wedding. The Princess's first official engagement was at a charity show held at Goldsmith's Hall, London in aid of the Royal Opera House, Covent Garden on 9th March (opposite, right). The Princess's stunning black silk taffeta dress was made by David and Elizabeth Emmanuel, the young designers chosen by Diana to make her wedding dress.

On 27th March, Charles and Diana visited Cheltenham Police HQ (above). Police from this force guard Highgrove House, Gloucestershire, one of the royal couple's residences. The same day, Charles and Diana, with the Queen, visited Dean Close School, Cheltenham, where 18-year-old Nicholas Hardy gallantly kissed the hand of his 'future Queen' (opposite, top left). The Prince and his new fiancée smile for the cameras before going into Clarence House for a private engagement party on 24th February (left).

Charles and Diana, accompanied by Princess Margaret, attended Sandown Park, Surrey on 13th March 1981 (below). The Prince's mount, Good Prospect, failed to live up to its name – it threw the Prince at the eighteenth fence in the Grand Military Gold Cup Chase.

A not so happy picture (opposite, bottom left) as a glum Prince Charles leaves Diana behind in London as he flies from Heathrow Airport on 29th March 1981 for New Zealand, the first stop on a four-nation tour due to last five weeks. 'A touching parting,' said observers.

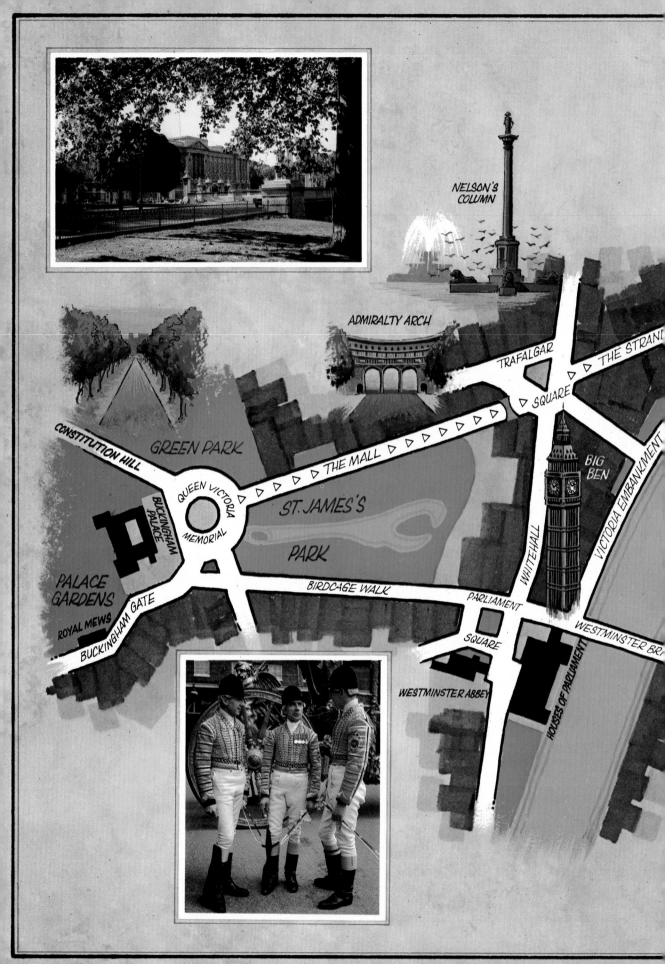

NELSON'S COLUMN

ADMIRALTY ARCH

TRAFALGAR
SQUARE

THE STRAND

CONSTITUTION HILL

GREEN PARK

THE MALL

BIG
BEN

BUCKINGHAM PALACE

QUEEN VICTORIA MEMORIAL

ST. JAMES'S

PARK

WHITEHALL

VICTORIA EMBANKMENT

PALACE
GARDENS

ROYAL MEWS

BUCKINGHAM GATE

BIRDCAGE WALK

PARLIAMENT

SQUARE

BUCKINGHAM

WESTMINSTER BR

WESTMINSTER ABBEY

HOUSES OF PARLIAMENT

LAW COURTS

ALDWYCH

SOMERSET HOUSE

FLEET STREET

LUDGATE CIRCUS

LUDGATE HILL

ST. PAULS CATHEDRAL

WATERLOO BRIDGE

H.M.S. DISCOVERY

CLEOPATRA'S NEEDLE

RIVER THAMES

BLACKFRIARS BRIDGE

Processional Route

29th July 1981 was a day of great celebrations, not only in the capital but all over Britain, and for British people all over the world.

The royal procession from St Paul's passed down Fleet Street and the Strand through Trafalgar Square and down the Mall to Buckingham Palace. The entire route was lined with excited crowds, all cheering, waving Union Jacks and vying for a glimpse of their charming Prince of Wales and his beautiful Princess.

Few Archbishops of Canterbury perform the wedding ceremony of the heir to the throne. The last Prince of Wales to marry was Queen Victoria's heir, later King Edward VII, in 1863. A rare task therefore falls to the present, 102nd Archbishop of Canterbury, Robert Runcie, who became Primate of All England, and leader of 70,000,000 Anglicans throughout the world, only in 1980. The pictures, (left and below), show him at his enthronement in Canterbury Cathedral on 25th March and (above) relaxing afterwards outside the cathedral.

Top left, some of this crowd have waited three days to see the wedding procession pass along Ludgate Hill. Top right, patience rewarded: here comes the bridegroom: Prince Charles in the uniform of a Royal Navy Commander, with Prince Andrew, as Midshipman. Andrew has the ring. Bottom, the two Princes mount the red-carpeted stairs into St Paul's Cathedral, passing the bearskinned mixed Armed Services guard of honour. The bride, the soon-to-be Princess of Wales, is five minutes behind and everything's on time.

*This page: two of the five
bridesmaids arriving at St Paul's
Cathedral. Right, Clementine
Hambro, and below, Catherine
Cameron. Opposite (inset), the
bridegroom's sister, Princess
Anne, and his aunt, Princess
Margaret, in the third carriage,
which also carried Anne's
husband, Captain Mark Phillips
and Margaret's son, Viscount
Linley. The wedding day
followed an important day for the
Phillips family: the christening of
their two-month old daughter
Zara, on 28th July. Opposite
below, the Queen, Prince Philip
and the Queen Mother are greeted
by the Archbishop of Canterbury
and dignitaries of St Paul's. In
the doorway, carnation in
buttonhole, stands Prince
Edward, third son of the
Queen.*

Right, here comes the bride smiling behind her veil, seated next to her father, Earl Spencer. Opposite left, Prince Philip exchanges a word with the Queen Mother. Below, the wedding dress of the year, the best kept secret of 1981, revealed at last. Huge puffed sleeves, wide, full skirt, antique lace trimming – and an 8-metre train spread out majestically behind the bride, as she emerges from the Glass Coach, which was drawn from Clarence House to St Paul's by two Bay horses, Lady Penelope and Kestrel. Opposite right, the bride, carrying a magnificent bouquet of cream and white flowers, with traditional myrtle and veronica from Osborne House, walks up the aisle on the arm of her father.

Left, Earl Spencer has escorted his youngest daughter to her royal bridegroom, with the bridesmaids and pages in attendance. Facing Earl Spencer, Lady Diana and Prince Charles, to their left is the Archbishop of Canterbury, Dr Robert Runcie, who is about to perform the marriage ceremony. Below, bride and groom kneel before the Archbishop during the marriage service. The promise to 'obey', given by the bride, was omitted, since the couple chose the alternative form of service established in the Church of England in 1927. Amid all the pomp and solemnity, the couple showed very human evidence of nerves. She got his names, Charles Philip Arthur George, muddled up. He forgot to say 'worldly' when he promised: '. . . and all my worldly goods with thee I share.'

In the foreground, backs to the camera, are Charles' grandmother, the Queen Mother, and his father Prince Philip, the Duke of Edinburgh. Alongside the bride: her parents, Earl Spencer and Mrs Shand Kydd, and her younger brother, Viscount Althorp, also named Charles.

Left, the Prince of Wales and his new Princess turn away from the altar to start their long walk back down the aisle. It's the first time in 118 years that Britain has had a Princess of Wales, since Prince Edward, afterwards King Edward the Seventh, married the Danish Princess Alexandra in 1863, and the first time a royal prince has married 'someone British' – which Charles very much wanted to do – since 1660. Below, down the long, long aisle of St Paul's Cathedral go the bride and groom. It takes 3½ minutes to traverse. Behind the royal newlyweds, the five bridesmaids, Clementine Hambro, Catherine Cameron, Sarah Jane Gaselee and India Hicks, and at the back with Prince Andrew and Prince Edward, Lady Sarah Armstrong-Jones, Princess Margaret's daughter. The two small pages (third row) are Edward van Cutsem and Lord Nicholas Windsor, son of the Duke of Kent.

Below, nearing the door of St Paul's, the Prince and Princess about to pass the Yeoman of the Guard, the famous 'Beefeaters'. Bottom, the carriage awaits and so do the jubilant crowds. The marriage service was relayed to them as they waited and their cheers could be heard inside St Paul's as the service proceeded. Right, the ride back to Buckingham Palace for the wedding breakfast, the Prince and Princess acknowledge the greetings of the well-wishers

packing the pavements, with the Lifeguards forming a spectacular escort. Opposite, just married and their smiles say it all. Now, the crowds can see that dress, and the Spencer family diamond tiara worn by the new Princess. These and all the other pictures of the Royal Wedding went round the world, with an estimated 500 million people watching on television. About 250,000 extra visitors were in London to join the celebrations on Royal Wedding Day.

Inset opposite, the triumphant ride from St Paul's is nearly over. The Prince and Princess drive through the gates of Buckingham Palace and (opposite) prepare to go inside for the wedding breakfast. Left, the crowd waits for the traditional balcony appearance. Centre, only a kiss apart, the newlyweds framed in the balcony window, as the royals come out to greet the cheering crowds. Bottom, leaving for the honeymoon, the carriage decorated with heart-shaped blue and silver balloons with the Prince's crest. At the back: 'Just Married'.

The Princess of Wales

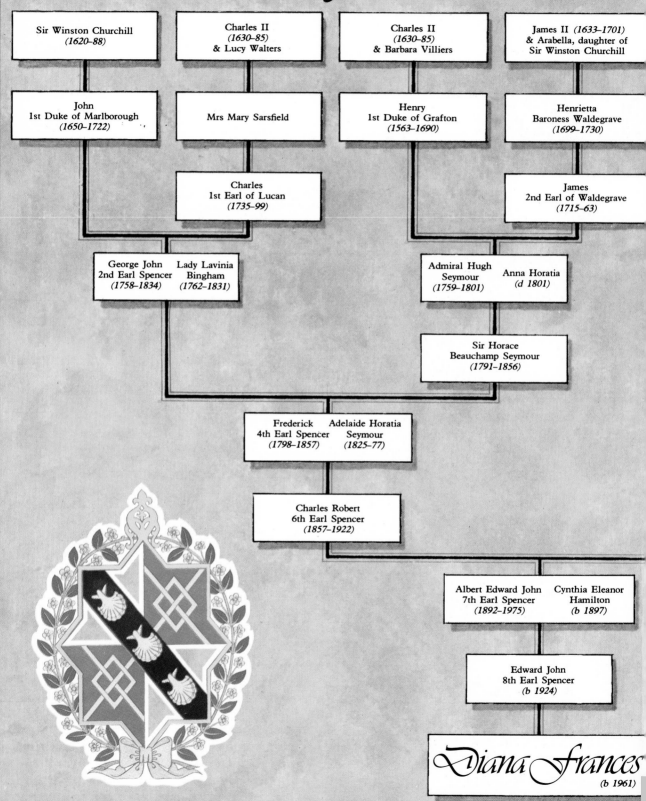

Sir Winston Churchill
(1620–88)

Charles II
(1630–85)
& Lucy Walters

Charles II
(1630–85)
& Barbara Villiers

James II *(1633–1701)*
& Arabella, daughter of
Sir Winston Churchill

John
1st Duke of Marlborough
(1650–1722)

Mrs Mary Sarsfield

Henry
1st Duke of Grafton
(1563–1690)

Henrietta
Baroness Waldegrave
(1699–1730)

Charles
1st Earl of Lucan
(1735–99)

James
2nd Earl of Waldegrave
(1715–63)

George John   Lady Lavinia
2nd Earl Spencer   Bingham
(1758–1834)   *(1762–1831)*

Admiral Hugh
Seymour   Anna Horatia
(1759–1801)   *(d 1801)*

Sir Horace
Beauchamp Seymour
(1791–1856)

Frederick   Adelaide Horatia
4th Earl Spencer   Seymour
(1798–1857)   *(1825–77)*

Charles Robert
6th Earl Spencer
(1857–1922)

Albert Edward John   Cynthia Eleanor
7th Earl Spencer   Hamilton
(1892–1975)   *(b 1897)*

Edward John
8th Earl Spencer
(b 1924)

Diana Frances
(b 1961)